The Basics of Front-End Web Development (HTML, CSS, and JavaScript)

By: Roggie Clark

Copyright

Title: The Basics of Front-End Web Development
Author: Roggie Clark

Cover Design: Roggie Clark
Editing: Renee' Clark

Printed in the United States of America

Disclaimer

The views and opinions expressed in this book are those of the author and do not necessarily reflect the official policy or position of any individual, company, or organization cited or referenced in the text.

The author is not affiliated with any of the individuals, companies, or organizations mentioned in the text, nor does the author receive any form of compensation for citing or referencing them. Some sample scenarios in this text are fictitious. Any similarity to actual persons, living or dead, is coincidental.

The professional information (strategies, tips, and concepts) in this text is distributed on an "as is" basis, without warranty. While every precaution has been taken in the preparation of the text to ensure all information is accurate, neither the author nor the publisher shall have any liability to any person or entity with respect to any loss or damage caused or alleged to be caused directly or indirectly by the instructions contained in this text or by the computer software and hardware products described in it.

Neither the author nor the publisher guarantees any specific results or outcomes, and the information provided in this text should not be construed as professional advice. Readers should always consult with a qualified professional before making any significant changes to their website or business.

By reading this text, you agree that the author nor the publisher is responsible for any direct, indirect, incidental, or consequential damages that may arise from the use of the information provided. You assume full responsibility for any actions taken based on the information presented in this text.

Table of Contents

Chapter 1: Introduction to the Web – HTML, CSS, and JavaScript

Thank you for picking up this book to help advance your coding knowledge. In this book, we are exploring three fundamental technologies: **HTML**, **CSS**, and **JavaScript**. These languages, often referred to as the building blocks of the web, work together to create the websites we browse, complex web applications, and so much more.

By learning these foundational coding languages in detail, you can design, structure, and maintain websites, and thus be considered a novice *Front-End Web Developer*.

With technology becoming ever more noticeable in our daily lives, having this baseline knowledge is critical in becoming a well-versed I.T. professional.

So with that being said, before diving into more advanced topics, it's essential to have a firm grasp of what each of these components does and how they interconnect.

Below I included a quick introduction to each of the coding languages, this is meant to help you gain a base-line understanding of each before I dive into greater detail in the next few chapters. Let's start first with HTML.

HTML – The Structure of the Web

HTML, or **HyperText Markup Language**, forms the "backbone" of every webpage. Think of it as the skeleton of a website, providing structure and meaning to the content that's displayed. Every piece of visible content on a webpage – from headings and paragraphs to images and links – is defined using HTML.

HTML allows you to create a hierarchy of "elements". These elements help browsers understand how to display the content. For instance, headings tell the browser (and the user) that a section of text is important, while paragraphs and lists organize information into readable formats.

Without HTML, there would be no structure to websites. It's the foundation upon which all other web technologies are built. However, while HTML can describe what's on a webpage, it doesn't dictate how the page should look. This is where CSS comes in.

CSS – The Design of the Web

While HTML provides the structure, **CSS** or **Cascading Style Sheets**, is responsible for styling. It gives front-end developers the ability to control the appearance of a webpage, from colors and fonts to layouts and spacing. With CSS, you can transform a plain page of text into a visually appealing experience.

CSS works by targeting HTML elements and applying "styles" to them. You can choose everything from the size of text to the alignment of images and the overall layout of the page. Want your headings to be bold and blue? CSS makes that happen. Want to ensure the layout adapts to different screen sizes? CSS can handle that too.

In addition to colors and fonts, CSS is crucial for creating responsive designs – designs that adjust smoothly across different devices, whether someone is browsing on a smartphone, tablet, or desktop computer. As more people use a variety of devices to access the web, mobile responsive website design has become an essential part of modern web development. While CSS can create visually appealing web applications, unfortunately, it can't design a dynamic visual experience. For this you need another coding language, JavaScript.

JavaScript – The Behavior of the Web

While HTML provides structure and CSS controls design, **JavaScript** is what brings a website to life. JavaScript is a scripting language that enables interaction, allowing web pages to respond dynamically to user inputs.

Imagine filling out a form online. As you type, perhaps the website gives you instant feedback, highlighting errors or suggesting corrections. Or maybe you're browsing an online store, and items are dynamically updated in your shopping cart without needing to reload the entire page. This is JavaScript in action.

JavaScript gives websites the ability to perform complex tasks, like manipulating the content of the page in real-time, handling "events" (such as clicks or key presses), and fetching data from servers without refreshing the page. It's the engine behind many of the interactive elements that users have come to expect from modern web experiences.

Beyond enhancing interactivity, JavaScript also enables the creation of full-fledged web applications. From games and calculators to content management systems and beyond, JavaScript is a key player in building advanced functionality on the web.

Last Thoughts

In the following chapters, we'll explore each of these technologies in greater depth, helping you see how they form the foundation of the modern web. But for now, keep in mind that to create a fully functioning website, HTML, CSS, and JavaScript must work in harmony.

HTML structures the content, CSS styles it, and JavaScript makes it interactive. Each serves a distinct role, but together, they enable developers to build the websites and applications that make the World Wide Web such a rich, vibrant place.

Mastering these three languages is the first step towards becoming a capable web developer. Once you're comfortable with them, you'll have the skills to bring your ideas to lie on the web. This journey starts with understanding the fundamentals and gradually building more complex projects as you go.

Okay, with that being said let's explore the first coding language I discussed, and that is HTML.

Chapter 2: Hypertext Markup Language (HTML)

HyperText Markup Language (HTML) is the *standard markup* or computer code that is used to create and structure content on the web. Web browsers can "render" (display) HTML on a user's computer screen, in a format readable for the user. (Wikipedia, n.d.).

Created by Sir Timothy John Berners-Lee; HTML was designed, in 1989, as an easy-to-use and effective method for creating documents for the World Wide Web.

At the time the internet was still in its infancy stage, and there wasn't a clear way to create and structure content on web pages.

Users often would send *FTP (File Transfer Protocol)* files to each other to display their work online, but these files were often bulky, fragmented, and not searchable or accessible to other users.

HTML was able to address this issue by allowing developers to embed their content in the form of clickable text, or *hypertext,* which users can create using *elements* also sometimes referred to as *tags*.

Tags are specific pieces of code meant to represent the parts of the document. The tags are similar to the common features of a book, like titles, headers, paragraphs, lists, etc.

To make things even more accessible, users are also able to "link" or connect documents using *hyperlinks.* Over time HTML has evolved to include other elements but the same basic functionality remains today (Wikipedia, n.d.).

Here's an example of a basic HTML document (W3School, n.d.):

```
<!DOCTYPE html>
<html>
     <head>
           </head>
         <body>

         </body>
</html>
```

Key Components of An HTML Document

Let's break down this example into its components, as you can see, HTML documents include several key elements such as: <!DOCTYPE html>. This is the statement that declares that the document is an HTML document. All HTML documents must include this statement.

Additionally, The <!DOCTYPE html> declaration is used to inform the browser which version of HTML the page is written in. In modern web development, we use **HTML5**, and <!DOCTYPE html>is the declaration for HTML5.

Next is the <html> element, which defines the start of the HTML document, it "wraps" around everything that's displayed on a webpage. It marks the beginning and end of the document.

Next is the <head> element. This tag represents the top or beginning of the HTML document. Additionally, it may contain meta-information about the page. This can include the title, meta tags (used for search engine optimization), and links to external resources such as JavaScript and/or CSS files. It does not contain content that will be visible to users.

Lastly, the <body> section contains the actual content that will be displayed on the webpage. It includes text, images, links, buttons, and anything else users will interact with.

There are additional, HTML tags that you will commonly see but before doing that I believe that it is important to establish a baseline understanding of HTML syntax first.

HTML Syntax

When writing HTML it is important to know the proper way to do it, this ensures that your code is easy to read and follow. Here's what you should know about HTML syntax:

1. Closing Tags and Self-Closing Elements:

- Most elements have **opening** (<head>) and **closing** tags (</head>). The content goes between these tags. As you can see, the / is used to represent the closing tag.
- Some tags, like <img> or <br>, are **self-closing** and don't need a closing tag. (We explore what these tags represent in the *common HTML Tags* section)
- Always make sure to close your tags (for elements that require a closing tag) and use self-closing syntax for elements like <img> and <br>.

---

2. Not Case-Sensitive:

- HTML tags are **not case-sensitive**, but the convention is to write them in **lowercase** (e.g., <body>, not <Body> or <BODY>). This improves readability and consistency.

---

3. HTML Attributes:

- Attributes provide additional information about an element. They are always written in the **opening tag** and come in name/value pairs, like href="https://example.com" in an *anchor tag* (<a>). We will explore *anchor tags* in greater detail in the *common HTML Tags* section
- The attribute value should be enclosed in **double quotes** (" "), though single quotes (' ') are technically allowed.

Example:

<a href="https://example.com" target="_blank">Visit Example</a>

---

4. Nesting and Proper Tag Hierarchy:

- HTML elements can be **nested** inside one another. However, proper **tag hierarchy** is crucial.
- Always close tags in the **reverse order** in which they were opened.

As you can recall from the previous code snippet I showed above:

```
<!DOCTYPE html>
<html>
     <head>
           </head>
          <body>

          </body>
```

```
</html>
```

Inside of the <!DOCTYPE html> element, the <html> is nested inside of it, and then nested inside of it, is the <head> element, and nested inside the <html> element is the <body> element.

Here is an example of incorrect nesting:

```
<!DOCTYPE html>
<html>
     <head><body></body></head>
</html>
```

As you can see the <body> element is incorrectly nested in the <head> element.

---

5. Indentation and Readability:

- Use consistent **indentation** to organize nested elements. This improves the readability of the code, especially for larger documents.
- Typically, a **two or four-space** indentation is used for each level of nesting.

Again recalling the code snippet example from above, notice how each tag starts on a new “line” again this improves readability.

```
<!DOCTYPE html>
<html>
     <head>
           </head>
          <body>

          </body>
</html>
```

---

6. HTML Comments:

- Comments are helpful for leaving notes in the code for future reference. They do not affect how the webpage is displayed.

- Comments are added using the syntax: <!-- Comment -->.

Example:

<!-- This is a comment explaining the code -->

<head></head>

Now that we discussed how to write HTML properly, let's explore what are some common HTML elements that all novice front-end web developers should know.

Common HTML Tags

For novice front-end web developers, mastering common HTML tags is crucial to creating well-structured web pages. Here's a list of fundamental HTML tags every beginner should know:

1. Basic Structure Tags:

- <html>: The root element of an HTML document.
- <head>: Contains meta-information like title, styles, and scripts.
- <body>: Contains the content of the webpage (text, images, links, etc.).

---

2. Text and Content Tags:

- <h1> to <h6>: Header tags, with <h1> being the largest and usually the most important. Next is <h2> then <h3> next <h4>, <h5> and ending with <h6> as the smallest.
- <p>: Paragraph tag for blocks of text.
-
: Line break, creates a new line within text.
- <hr>: Horizontal rule, creates a horizontal line break.
- <strong>: Boldens text for emphasis (also conveys semantic meaning for search engine optimization).
- <em>: Italicizes text for emphasis (also conveys semantic meaning).

---

3. List Tags:

- <ul>: Unordered list (bulleted).
- <ol>: Ordered list (numbered).
- <li>: List item within <ul> or <ol>.

Additional Information On HTML List

To code an HTML list, you use different tags for ordered and unordered lists.

Unordered List (bulleted):

- Use the <ul> tag.

- Add list items inside it with the <li> tag.

Ordered List (numbered):

- Use the <ol> tag.

- Add list items inside it with the <li> tag.

Example:

Unordered List:

```
<ul>
  <li>Item 1</li>
  <li>Item 2</li>
  <li>Item 3</li>
</ul>
```

How it looks in HTML:

- Item 1
- Item 2
- Item 3

Ordered List:

```
<ol>
  <li>Item 1</li>
  <li>Item 2</li>
  <li>Item 3</li>
</ol>
```

How it looks in HTML:

1. Item 1
2. Item 2
3. Item 3

---

4. Link and Navigation Tags:

- <a>: Anchor tag for hyperlinks. Links to other pages or sections using the href attribute.
- <nav>: Defines a section for navigation links.

---

5. Media Tags:

- <img>: Embeds images using the src attribute to specify the image source.
- <video>: Embeds video content.
- <audio>: Embeds audio content.

---

6. Table Tags:

- <table>: Defines a table.

- <tr>: Table row.
- <td>: Table data (cell).
- <th>: Table header.

Additional Information On HTML Tables

HTML tables are a bit tricky to create so here's a bit of information on this. To code an HTML table, you use the <table> element and its child elements. Here's a quick guide:

1. Create the table using the <table> tag.

2. Define rows with <tr> (table row).

3. Add table headers using <th> (table header).

4. Add table data using <td> (table data cell).

Example:

```
<table>

 <tr>

  <th>Header 1</th>

  <th>Header 2</th>

  <th>Header 3</th>

 </tr>

 <tr>

  <td>Data 1</td>

  <td>Data 2</td>

  <td>Data 3</td>

 </tr>

 <tr>
```

```
  <td>Data 4</td>

  <td>Data 5</td>

  <td>Data 6</td>

 </tr>

</table>
```

This will create a basic table with a header row and two rows of data. An example of how the HTML will be displayed is below.

Header 1	Header 2	Header 3
Data 1	Data 2	Data 3
Data 4	Data 5	Data 6

---

7. Form Tags:

- <form>: Creates an HTML form for user input.
- <input>: Defines an input field (e.g., text, checkbox, radio, etc.).
- <button>: Button for submitting forms or performing actions.
- <label>: Label for form elements.
- <textarea>: Multi-line text input field.

---

8. Grouping Tags:

- <div>: Division or container for structuring content.it is also called a *block-level element* because it is displayed on one line, and pushes non-block elements below or to the side of the block element.
- <span>: Inline container for styling or grouping small sections of text.
- <id>: this attribute is used to point to a specific style declaration in a style sheet (we will explore *stylesheets* in the *How CSS is added to HTML section* of the *CSS chapter*). It is

also used by JavaScript (we will explore this in the *function section* of the *Javascript chapter*) to access and manipulate the element with the specific id.

---

10. Metadata Tags:

- <meta>: Provides metadata like character encoding, viewport settings, SEO tags. This tag is self closing.
- <link>: Links to external resources like stylesheets.

These tags form the foundation of HTML and are essential for structuring and presenting content on the web. Additionally, avoid deprecated elements. Some older HTML elements (like <font>or <center>) are **deprecated** in modern HTML5 and should not be used. Use **CSS** for styling and layout instead.

Semantic HTML Tags

Additionally, it is worth noting that since the introduction of HTML5, several other elements have been added. When structuring webpages you should:

- Use **semantic elements** (like `<article>`, `<section>`, etc.) to describe the content's structure and purpose. Instead of (`<div>` and `<span>` which don't tell anything about the content on the page.)
- Additionally, Semantic HTML helps enhance the document's readability, accessibility, and SEO-friendliness.

Example:

```
<article>
  <header>
    <h1>Understanding Semantic HTML</h1>
  </header>
  <p>This article explains the importance of semantic HTML.</p>
</article>
```

Additional Semantic Tags (HTML5):

- **<header>**: Defines the header section of a webpage or section.

- <footer>: Defines the footer section.
- <section>: Groups-related content.
- <article>: Represents an independent piece of content.
- <aside>: Sidebar content related to the main content.
- <main>: The main content area of the document.

HTML Tags For SEO:

If you are familiar with SEO (search engine optimization), which if you are serious about creating websites, you should learn, there are additional tags/code snippets needed for optimal search engine performance, here they are:

- `<title>`This snippet is used to write a **Title tag** for the page, sometimes referred to as *Meta titles* or *Title links,* this tag is used by searchers to see what the name of the webpage is, and for some insight into what it is about, thus enticing them to click on the webpage.

- `<meta name="description" content="">`This snippet is used to write a **Meta Description** for the page. Similar to the Title Tag, the Meta description is to entice a reader to click on the webpage. Additionally, search engines use the meta description to explain to searchers what a webpage is about.

- `<meta name="robots" content="index, follow" >` This tag controls how search engines index and follow your page. A common value is index, follow, which allows search engines to index the page and follow its links.

- `<meta charset="UTF-8">` This code snippet indicates the *character encoding* or the types of symbols, and text used in the document. This matters because different languages have different symbols and characters, so using *UTF-8,* which is the standard that most search engines prefer, covers all of the possible characters used in any language.

- `<meta http-equiv="X-UA-Compatible" content="IE=edge">` This code snippet ensures that all Web browsers can properly display the document.

- `<meta name="viewport" content="width=device-width, initial-scale=1.0">` This code snippet ensures that the document is viewable on all devices, especially mobile devices.

HTML Attributes

In HTML, attributes provide additional information about elements. They are always written inside the opening tag and are made up of a **name** and a **value**. The **name** specifies what kind of information is being given, and the **value** provides the information itself. For example:

```
<a href="https://example.com">Visit Example</a>
```

In the above example, `href` is the attribute name, and `"https://example.com"` is the value. Attributes enhance elements by providing extra data or modifying behavior.

Structure of HTML Attributes

1. **Name**: The attribute name (e.g., `href`, `id`, `class`).
2. **Value**: The value for that attribute is provided in quotes (e.g., `"https://example.com", "header"`).

Attributes usually appear as **name-value pairs**, but some attributes are **boolean attributes** (such as `disabled`, `checked`, or `readonly`), which don't need a value but indicate the presence of a certain feature.

Common HTML Attributes

Here are the most commonly used HTML attributes that beginners should understand:

- `id`
  Defines a unique identifier for an element. Useful for targeting specific elements with CSS or JavaScript.

  ```
  <div id="header">This is the header</div>
  ```

- `class`
  Used to apply CSS styles or target multiple elements in JavaScript.

```
<p class="intro">This is an introduction.</p>
```

- `style`
  Used to apply inline CSS styles directly to an element.

```
<h1 style="color: red;">Red Heading</h1>
```

- `href`
  Specifies the URL for a link.

```
<a href="https://example.com">Click Here</a>
```

- `src`
  Defines the source of an image, video, or script.

```
<img src="image.jpg" alt="Sample Image">
```

- `alt`
  Provides alternative text for images. Important for accessibility and SEO.

```
<img src="logo.png" alt="Company Logo">
```

- `title`
  Adds extra information, often displayed as a tooltip when the user hovers over the element.

```
<p title="This is a paragraph.">Hover over this text.</p>
```

- `target`
  Specifies where to open a linked document. Common values include:
  - `_blank` (open in a new tab or window)
  - `_self` (default, opens in the same tab)

```
<a href="https://example.com" target="_blank">Open in New
Tab</a>
```

- `rel`
  Defines the relationship between the current document and the linked document. Often used with `href`.

```
<a href="https://example.com" rel="noopener">External
Link</a>
```

- `type`
  Specifies the type of an input field or script.

```
<input type="text" placeholder="Enter your name">
```

- `value`
  Defines the initial value for input elements like forms.

```
<input type="text" value="Default text">
```

- `placeholder`
  Provides a hint to users about what they can enter in an input field.

```
<input type="email" placeholder="Enter your email">
```

- `disabled`
  A boolean attribute that disables an element (e.g., a form input).

```
<button disabled>Submit</button>
```

- `readonly`
  Makes input fields non-editable, while still allowing them to be focused and copied.

```
<input type="text" value="Read only" readonly>
```

- `checked`
  A boolean attribute used with checkboxes or radio buttons to indicate a default selected option.

```
<input type="checkbox" checked> I agree to the terms
```

- `name`
  Specifies a name for input elements, allowing them to be identified when the form is submitted.

```
<input type="text" name="username">
```

- `action`
  Defines where the form data should be sent when submitted (usually a URL).

```
<form action="/submit-form" method="post">
```

- `method`
  Specifies how to send form data: either `GET` (for URL parameters) or `POST` (for more secure data submission).

```
<form action="/submit-form" method="post">
```

- `maxlength`
  Limits the number of characters a user can input.

```
<input type="text" maxlength="10">
```

- `data-*`
  Custom data attributes allow you to store extra information in an element, often used in JavaScript.

```
<div data-user-id="123">User Information</div>
```

How Attributes Work Together

Attributes often work in combination. For example, a form input field might include several attributes to specify its behavior:

```
<input type="text" name="username" placeholder="Enter your
username" maxlength="20" required>
```

In this example:

- `type="text"` specifies that this is a text input.
- `name="username"` gives the field a name.
- `placeholder="Enter your username"` provides a hint to the user.
- `maxlength="20"` limits the input to 20 characters.
- `required` ensures that the field must be filled before submitting the form.

Final Thoughts

Attributes are the building blocks of HTML elements, providing important metadata and controlling how elements behave or appear. Understanding these common attributes will allow you to enhance your HTML structure for better design, interactivity, and accessibility.

Last Words About Hypertext Markup Language (HTML)

The key thing to remember about HTML is that it is a way to construct the different parts of a web page and make them functional for web browsers. This is the reason why it is so widely used.

It is also the reason why search engines define the bulk of their algorithm ranking factors around ensuring that they send users to websites that have well-structured HTML pages.

In the next chapter, we'll explore CSS, the language that brings style and design to your HTML elements.

Chapter 3: Cascading Style Sheets (CSS)

Co-created by Norwegian web developer Håkon Wium Lie and Dutch computer scientist Bert Bos, **Cascading Style Sheets (CSS)** was released in 1996 as a new programming language used to "style" or change the appearance of HTML elements, to make them more visually appealing to the reader (Wikipedia, n.d.).

With CSS, you can control many aspects of the look and feel of an HTML webpage including text size, text color, font type, background color, borders, margins, etc.

The instructions that the browsers use to accurately display the style of these elements are stored in documents called "Stylesheets". The name "Cascading" comes from the ability of one style sheet to inherit or overwrite the styles of another or *Cascade* (Hoffman, 2017).

CSS is considered to be a "declarative" programming language, meaning that it gives the web browser *suggestions* on how to display the elements on the webpage; but does not assert *exactly* how to display them. (Britannica, n.d.). This unique functionality of CSS makes it one of the most widely used tools in web design and development today.

CSS Syntax

Just like HTML, to write CSS properly, there are a few things you should consider, following these syntax rules will ensure that your code is correct, easy to read, and can be used multiple times. Here are the syntax rules:

1. CSS Syntax Structure:

CSS consists of two main components: **selectors** and **declarations**.

- A **selector** identifies the HTML element you want to style.
- A **declaration** specifies the style to be applied.

Declarations are written inside **curly braces** `{ }` and consist of a **property** and a **value**, separated by a colon (`:`). Each declaration ends with a semicolon (`;`).

Basic Structure of CSS:

```
selector {
  property: value;
}
```

Example:

```
h1 {
  color: blue;
  font-size: 24px;
}
```

In this example:

- `h1` is the selector (it targets all `<h1>` elements).
- `color: blue;` is a declaration that changes the text color to blue.
- `font-size: 24px;` sets the font size to 24 pixels.

---

2. Selectors and Specificity:

- Different types of **Selectors** can also be used to determine which HTML elements get styled. Common types include:
  - **Type selectors** (e.g., `p`) target elements by name.
  - **Class selectors** (e.g., `.classname`) target elements with a specific class. The `.` is used to indicate that a class selector is being used.
  - **ID selectors** (e.g., `#idname`) target elements with a unique ID. The `#` is used to indicate that an ID selector is being used.
- **Specificity** determines which style is applied if multiple rules conflict:
  - IDs have higher specificity than classes, which have higher specificity than type selectors.
  - Inline styles `(style="...")` have the highest specificity. (we will explore inline styles in greater detail in the *How CSS is Added to HTML Section.*

---

3. Cascading and Inheritance:

- As I said earlier, CSS stands for **Cascading Style Sheets** because the styles "cascade" down. Because of this, if multiple rules apply to an element, the rule with the highest specificity or the rule declared last takes precedence. So if the rule is an ID it will take precedence over a Class. While a Class would take precedence over a Type.
- Some properties are **inherited** `(e.g., font-family)`, meaning they are passed down from parent elements to child elements. Others, like `margin` or `border`, are not

inherited. We will explore these properties in greater detail in the *Common CSS Properties* section

---

4. Box Model:

- Every HTML element can be thought of as a **box**. Understanding the **box model** is crucial for layout. The box consists of **content**, **padding**, **border**, and **margin,** below I included an image of what the box model looks like, this will help you with using it**:**

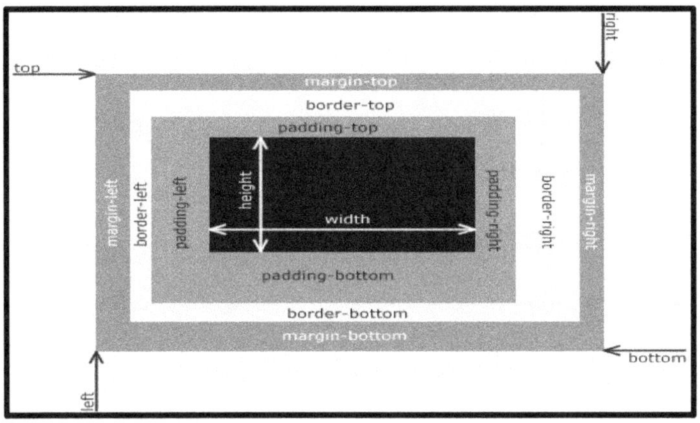

Cite:https://en.wikipedia.org/wiki/CSS_box_model

Example:

```
article {

  margin: 10px;

  padding: 20px;

  border: 1px solid black;

}
```

---

5. Units and Measurements:

- CSS uses a variety of units for lengths and sizes:
  - **Pixels** (`px`) are fixed units. For example, `10px`
  - **Percentages** (`%`) are relative to a parent container's size. E.g `10%`

- **Ems** (`em`) and **rem** are relative units based on font size (useful for responsive design). E.g `10em` or `1rem`
- For responsive designs, relative units like `%`, `em`, and `rem` are preferred over fixed `px`.

---

6. Shorthand Properties:

- CSS has many **shorthand properties** that allow you to set multiple values at once, reducing the amount of code you write.

Example:

```
/* Longhand */

margin-top: 10px;

margin-right: 20px;

margin-bottom: 10px;

margin-left: 20px;


/* Shorthand */

margin: 10px 20px;
```

---

7. Pseudo Classes:

A **CSS pseudo-class** is a keyword added to selectors that specifies a special state of an element. Pseudo-classes are used to style elements based on dynamic factors like user interaction or position within the document, even though they might not be distinguishable through standard attributes.

For example, a pseudo-class can apply styles when:

- The user hovers over a link (`:hover`)
- A form input is focused (`:focus`)
- A link has been visited (`:visited`)

- The first child of an element is selected (`:first-child`)

Here's an example of using the `:hover` pseudo-class to change the color of a link when a user hovers over it:

```
a:hover {

  color: red;

}
```

In this case, when the user moves the mouse over a link, its color will change to red. Pseudo-classes are very useful for creating interactive designs and improving the user experience without requiring JavaScript.

---

8. Commenting:

- Comments in CSS are written with `/* */` and can help make your code more readable and easier to maintain.

Example:

```
/* This styles the heading */

h1 {

  color: blue; }
```

Common CSS Properties

Now that we explored CSS syntax in detail let's now go over other examples of common CSS properties you may encounter:

1. Color and Background:

- `color`: Sets the text color. **Example:** `{color: #333;}`
- `background-color`: Specifies the background color of an element. **Example:** `{background-color: #f5f5f5;}`

- `background-image:` Adds an image as the background of an element. Be sure to add url of the image you wish to add. **E.g;** `background-image: url('image.jpg');`

---

2. Typography:

- `font-family:` Specifies the font type.
  Example: `{font-family: 'Arial', sans-serif;}`

- `font-size:` Defines the size of the text.
  Example: `{font-size: 16px;}`

- `font-weight:` Controls the boldness of the text.
  Example: `{font-weight: bold;}`

- `text-align:` Aligns text horizontally (left, center, right). **Example:** `{text-align: center;}`

- `line-height:` Controls the space between lines of text. **Example:** `{line-height: 1.5;}`

---

3. Spacing:

- `margin:` Defines the space outside the element.
  Example: `{margin: 20px;}`

- `padding:` Defines the space inside the element, between the content and the border.
  Example: `{padding: 15px;}`

---

4. Box Model:

- `width:` **and** `height:` Set the width and height of an element.
  Example: `{width: 300px;`

```
height: 200px;
}
```

- `border`: Adds a border around an element.
  Example: `{border: 1px solid #000;}`

- `border-radius`: sets the roundness of corners on the border
  Example: `{border-radius: 50px 20px;}`

- `box-shadow`: Adds shadow around an element.
  Example: `{border: 1px solid #000;}`

---

5. Positioning:

- `position`: Specifies the positioning method (static, relative, absolute, fixed).
  Example: `{position: relative;}`

- `top, right, bottom, left`: Offsets an element from its position.
  Example: `{top: 10px; left: 20px;}`

---

6. Display and Layout:

- `display`: Defines how an element is displayed (block, inline, inline-block, flex).
  Example:
  ```
  {display: block;
  display: flex;
  }
  ```

- `flex`: Enables flexbox layout properties for easier element alignment.
  Example: `{display: flex; justify-content: space-between;}`

- `overflow`: Controls how overflowed content is handled (visible, hidden, scroll).
  Example: `{overflow: hidden;}`

---

7. Visibility:

- `visibility:` Controls the visibility of an element (visible, hidden).
  Example: `{visibility: hidden;}`

- `opacity:` Sets the opacity (transparency) of an element.
  css
  Example: `{opacity: 0.5;}`

---

8. Hover Effects:

- `:hover`: Adds styles to an element when the mouse hovers over it.
  Example: `a:hover { color: red;}`

Mobile Responsive Design

Producing websites that work seamlessly across mobile devices is now a requirement for a skilled developer in this age. The reason being, search engines only want to send users to websites that are "Mobile responsive".

This matters greatly for SEO, and again to be a great web developer you should definitely learn SEO. So reading this section will help you do it. Let's get into it;

1. Fluid Layouts:

- **Use Relative Units**: Instead of fixed units like `px` , use flexible units like percentages `(%)`, `em` , `rem` , or viewport-based units (`vw`, `vh`) for width, margin, padding, etc. This helps elements adapt to different screen sizes.

Example:

```
.container {

    width: 80%; /* Adapts to the size of the viewport */

}
```

---

2. Media Queries:

- **Adjust Layout Based on Screen Size**: Use media queries to apply different styles for various screen widths. This allows you to design for specific device sizes (mobile, tablet, desktop).

Example:
```
@media only screen and (max-width: 768px) {

    .container {

        width: 100%;

        padding: 10px;

    }

}
```

---

3. Mobile-First Approach:

- **Design for Small Screens First**: Start by designing for mobile devices, then use media queries to scale up for larger screens. This ensures that the essential content is optimized for smaller, more restrictive devices.

Example:
```
/* Default (mobile-first) */

body { font-size: 16px; }



/* For tablets and small desktops */

@media (min-width: 768px) and (max-width: 1024px)

{ body { font-size: 18px; }
```

```
/* For large desktops and up */

@media (min-width: 1025px)

{ body { font-size: 20px; } }
```

---

4. Flexible Grid Systems:

- **CSS Grid or Flexbox**: Use these layout systems to create flexible and adaptive grid structures that rearrange themselves based on screen size.

  Below I include an image that I cited showing the difference between a Flexbox and CSS Grid. As you can see the Flexbox is more "one-dimensional" this is for more archaic, static web pages. But with a grid, you can create dynamic layouts that adjust to different screen sizes, this is going to be more important for web app designing.

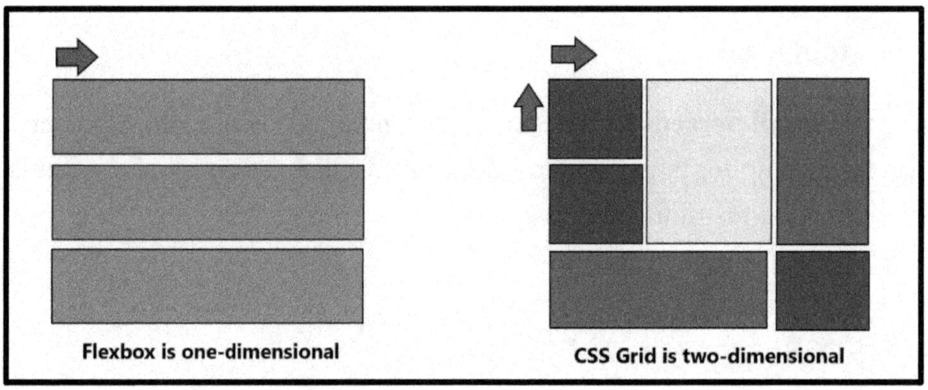

Cited:https://www.linkedin.com/pulse/revolutionizing-web-layouts-impact-flexbox-css-grid-razal-kabeer-qr0kf/

Flexbox Example:

```
.container {

    display: flex;

    flex-wrap: wrap;
```

```
}

.item {
    flex: 1 1 100%;
}

@media (min-width: 600px) {
    .item {
        flex: 1 1 50%;
    }
}
```

CSS Grid Example:

```
.grid {
    display: grid;
    grid-template-columns: 1fr;
}

@media (min-width: 768px) {
    .grid {
        grid-template-columns: 1fr 1fr;
    }
}
```

5. Viewport Meta Tag:

- **Set the Viewport for Mobile Devices**: Use the viewport meta tag in the HTML to ensure the browser adjusts the layout properly for mobile screens. If you recall from the *HTML Chapter* this tag is pivotal to having an optimal search engine performance as well, so don't forget it.

Example:

```
<meta name="viewport" content="width=device-width, initial-scale=1.0">
```

---

6. Responsive Images:

- **Use** `max-width` **for Images**: Ensure images resize proportionally by setting a `max-width` of 100% so they don't overflow their container.

Example:

```
img {

    max-width: 100%;

    height: auto;

}
```

---

7. Hide/Show Content:

- **Display or Hide Elements**: Sometimes, you may need to hide certain elements on smaller screens or show alternative content. You can use media queries to control visibility.

Example:

```
.desktop-only {

    display: none;
```

```
}

@media (min-width: 1024px) {

    .desktop-only {

        display: block;

    }

}
```

---

8. Test on Different Devices:

- **Cross-Device Testing**: Always test your site on different devices or use responsive design tools in browsers to ensure your styles work well across different screen sizes.

---

9. Touch-Friendly Elements:

- **Larger Clickable Areas**: Ensure that buttons, links, and interactive elements are large enough and spaced adequately for touch screens. Search engines like Google recommend a minimum touch target size of **48x48 pixels**.

---

10. CSS Frameworks (Optional):

- **Use CSS Frameworks**: "CSS frameworks" come with built-in responsive design utilities, grid systems, and pre-designed components that can help accelerate development. However, it's beneficial to understand the underlying principles before relying heavily on frameworks.

Final Thoughts

Understanding these properties will help you as a beginner create well-structured and visually appealing websites, while also providing a solid foundation to build more advanced designs. In the next section, we are going to explore the different ways in which CSS can be added to an HTML document.

How CSS is Added to HTML

CSS can be added to an HTML document generally in three ways: *inline, external,* or *internal*. Each way has pros and cons.

For the explanation of the pros and cons of each, I will be citing web author's; Nikita Hlopov article; *How to include CSS to a page (with Pros and Cons)*.

Inline CSS

For CSS to be added inline, the *style attribute* `style=""` or a special modifier that allows the CSS file to be referenced is added to the HTML tag or element.
Here's an example from W3school (n.d.):

```
<h1 style="color:blue;">insert text here</h1>
```

As you can see the code snippet includes the HTML element that is to be styled, this is also known as the *selector*. In this case, we are styling the <h1> element. Then an equal sign `=` and quotation marks "" are added to show that you are including a *declaration* that tells the computer to use the style defined in quotation marks.

Next, a *property* is added, which is the name of the style you want to use.

In the code example above, the property is `color` (change the font color).

The property is then followed by a colon `:`, then the *value* or what you want to change the element to.

For color, I wrote `blue`. Lastly, you end the declaration statement with a semicolon `;`

Also as you can see the style modifier is only added to the opening tag `<h1>`, this modifier should never be added to the closing tag `</h1>`

Pros and Cons

Here are some pros and cons of inline CSS implementation according to (Hlopov, 2021):

Pros:

- Useful for overriding default styling
- Has a higher specificity than any CSS selector (recall this information from the *CSS syntax section*; inline styles are more specific than **ID**, which is more specific than **Class**, which is more specific than **Type**. Also note this can be a Con because it can override more general styling and external stylesheets.

Cons:

- Not an easy way to apply styling for the whole page, especially if it's large
- Has a higher specificity than any CSS selector which can override external stylesheets
- Hard to manage and maintain.

External CSS

CSS can also be applied through an *external* file with the **.CSS** extension and then load it within a web page with an `<link>` HTML tag, and a `rel` and `href` attribute added to the link tag.

Here's an example:

```
<head>
  <link rel="stylesheet" href="styles.css">
</head>
```

As you can see the code; `<link rel="stylesheet" href="styles.css">` was nested in `<head>` tag.

The `<link>` tag indicates that a file is being called or located from another document. The `rel` attribute is used to indicate what type of file is to be requested, in this case a `stylesheet`. Then the `href` attribute indicates the name of the stylesheet file in this case, `styles.css` (W3school, n.d.).

You may be wondering, what does the `styles.css` file look like?

Here's a `styles.css` code snippet:

```
h1 {
  color: red;
}
```

In the code snippet, you can also see the HTML element that is to be styled. Again, in this case, the selector is added, `<h1>` element, followed by curly brackets `{ }` to indicate the start of the declaration. The `color` property is again added.

Then the property is again followed by a colon `:` then the "value" or what you want the property to be is added. For color, I added `red` and then ended the declaration statement with a semicolon `;`

Now, here are the pros and cons of using external CSS, according to (Hlopov, 2021):

Pros and Cons

Pros:

- All styles are stored in one separate file, making it easier to manage and maintain;
- Ability to include multiple different files if needed;
- Comments can be added to be interpretation easier for different developers
- The CSS file can be minified meaning decreased size in bytes. (This matters for SEO)

Cons:

- Linking external files creates render-blocking content which affects the rate and speed that Search engines can crawl and index web pages. Additionally, this can lead to a poor user experience because it may take visitors longer to access the website (Again this matters for SEO).

- May contain styles that are not used on a particular page, thus loading unused code. Which again can slow the rate and speed at which the website can be accessed and crawled by search engines.

Internal CSS

Lastly, we have internal CSS. Internal CSS is deployed using the `<style>` element nested in the `<head>` tag, again if you recall the `<head>` tag is generally where non-viewable/ non-interactive web elements are stored.

Next, nested in the `<style>` element is the *selector* or the element name that is to be styled is then included, in this case, it is the H2 tag `<h2>` again followed by curly brackets `{ }` to indicate the start of a declaration and then the property you want to style.

Here's an example:

```
<head>
     <style>
          H2 {
               Color: green;
               font-family: times new roman

               font-weight: bold;
               }
     </style>
</head>
```

In the code example, there are two new properties: `font-family` (changes the font type), and `font-weight` (Changes the thinness or thickness of the font).

The declaration is then followed by a colon **:**, then the value or what you want the property to be is added.

For `color`, I wrote `green`, for `font-family`, I wrote `times new roman`, and for `font-weight`, I wrote `bold`, to indicate I want the font to be thick. You end the declaration statement with a semicolon `;`

Now, let's review the pros and cons, again to recall (Hlopov, 2021):

Pros and Cons

Pros:

- Useful for overriding default styling;
- Can be turned on and off with JavaScript;
- Can be used to contain default minimum styling if the main stylesheet is being loaded asynchronously.

Cons:

- Not a very convenient way to apply styling for the whole page, especially if it's large;
- Hard to manage and maintain.

Last Words About Cascading Style Sheets (CSS)

CSS is a language used to tell web browsers *how* to display a website, and that it can be added to an HTML document in a variety of ways. Here are some additional tips for writing/ using CSS:

- **Keep it DRY (Don't Repeat Yourself)**: Reuse styles through classes and avoid redundant rules.
- **Organize your CSS**: Group related styles, use comments, and follow a logical order (e.g., start with base styles, then layout, then components).
- **Use external CSS files**: For better maintainability and separation of concerns, link external CSS files instead of inline styles.

By keeping these concepts in mind, you'll write CSS that is both efficient and easy to maintain. These foundational practices will also help you as you move into more advanced topics like layout systems (Flexbox, Grid) and responsive design as you continue to grow your knowledge base.

I also do want to mention that you may not have to physically write CSS yourself, as most CMSs (Content Management Systems) have an “interface” that allows you to write CSS without manipulating the code directly.

However, I do believe that it is important to know what it is and how it can be used if you want more control over how a website is displayed.

Now let’s explore the last and final coding language, and that is JavaScript.

Chapter 4: JavaScript

JavaScript is a versatile, high-level programming language developed by Brendan Eich, in 1995 as a way to make static HTML web pages more interactive. It is not to be confused with *Java,* despite similar names, they vary greatly in their purpose and usage.

JavaScript is used to create interactive, and dynamic effects on a web page, that happen based on user interactions like clicks, typing, scrolling, and more.

These effects can be things such as *pop-up ads*, animations, and much more (Eich and Dahl, n.d.). If you've ever used a form that instantly warns you about incorrect data without refreshing the page or a button that opens a dropdown menu, that's JavaScript at work.

Properties

What makes JavaScript unique from other programming languages is it is read and interpreted in the user's web browser during execution, as opposed to being compiled ahead of time and run by a separate application like *Java.*

This is why JavaScript is referred to as an **Interpreted** *or* **Just In Time (JIT) compiling language** (Doglio, 2020). This is often considered to be a good thing because it makes it easier for browsers to interpret and execute it.

JavaScript is generally run **synchronously**, which means the browser runs the code in the order in which it is written. It can also be run **asynchronously**, so if the code takes longer to execute, it will not block other parts of the document from being displayed.

This is important because it gives web developers the ability to make dynamic web pages that update automatically as the user interacts with the page.

Syntax

JavaScript Syntax or the unique set of rules the code must follow in order to be interpreted correctly by the browser. There are several key parts to JavaScript Syntax.

- First, it is case-sensitive, meaning changing the case of a letter can change the syntax of the code. For example, ***`FirstName`*** is not interpreted the same as ***`firstname`*** the browser would instead interpret these pieces of code as two different variables.

- Also, JavaScript uses a **unicode character set** which means developers have access to letters, numbers, and symbols from any language.

- Additionally, JavaScript statements are sometimes ended with a **semicolon** ; but this practice has fallen out of style in the programming community.

Here are the additional key components of JavaScript syntax;**Variables, Data Types, Operators, Statements**, **Expressions**, **Functions**, **DOM Manipulation, Events, Conditional Statements**, **Loops,** and **Comments**.

Values

In JavaScript, **Values** can be thought of as pieces or chunks of information that are assigned to different numbers or pieces of text (Haverbeke, 2018).

In JavaScript syntax, two of the most common values are **Literals** and **Variables**. (W3School, n.d.)

- **Fixed values** - Literals
- **Changeable values** - Variables

Literals

Fixed values are also referred to as **Literals**, they are called "fixed values" because they are values that generally are not changed, once they are declared they remain as such. They can be **Numbers** written either with or without decimals like:

```
9.20
```

```
9001
```

Or **Strings** which are text, written within double or single quotes:

```
"John Doe"
```

```
'John Doe'
```

Both types of values can be used to store pieces of information. There are additional *Data Types* like **Boolean, Array, Objects,** and **symbols,** which are standalone entities or things with their own identity and properties. We will explore *Data Types* in more detail in its own section.

Each of these can be used to represent values as well, but Fixed values and strings are the most simplistic, and can help you establish a foundation for exploring more intricate values in the future.

Variables

As I mentioned**, Variables** are changeable values. A Variable can be declared using var, let, and const keywords, according to (Tutorialsteacher, .n.d.):

- var is a more archaic way to define a JavaScript variable. It has fallen out of use because it can cause confusion with other JavaScript keywords, and it has limited usage due to scoping issues.
- let removes the confusion and error of var. It is the new and recommended way of declaring variables in JavaScript.
- const is used to declare a constant variable that cannot be changed once assigned a value.

Variables can also be thought of as digital containers for holding Literal values. Revisiting the last example here are variables written with numbers (W3School, n.d.):

```
var x = 5;

let y = 6;

const z = x + y;
```

As you can see, the keywords `var,` `let`, and `const`, are used to designate variables. Additionally in the code snippet; **operators** are used to perform mathematical and logical operations between variables, as you can see the operators `=` and `+` were used. I will explain this concept and the code snippet in more detail in the next section.

Data Types

As I mentioned, in addition to Numbers, Literal Values and Variables can be represented by different *Data Types* like:

1. String:

A sequence of characters, used to represent text.

Example:

```
let greeting = "Hello, World!";
console.log(greeting); // Output: Hello, World!
```

---

2. Number:

Represents both integer and floating-point numbers, i.e. digits like 123

Example:

```
let age = 30;
let pi = 3.14;
console.log(age); // Output: 30
console.log(pi);  // Output: 3.14
```

---

3. Boolean:

Represents logical entities, having only two values: `true` or `false`.

Example:

```
let isDeveloper = true;
console.log(isDeveloper); // Output: true
```

---

4. Array:

An ordered list of values, or that can be referenced by name i.e. a collection of items (indexed elements).

Example:

```
let colors = ["red", "green", "blue"];
console.log(colors[1]); // Output: green
```

---

5. Object:

A collection of key-value pairs.

Example:

```
let person = {
  name: "Alice",
  age: 25,
  isStudent: false
};
console.log(person.name); // Output: Alice
```

---

6. Symbol:

A unique and immutable primitive value, often used as a key in object properties.

Example:

```
let sym = Symbol("uniqueKey");
let obj = {
  [sym]: "value"
};
console.log(obj[sym]); // Output: value
```

---

7. Undefined:

A variable that has been declared but not yet assigned a value.

Example:

```
let notAssigned;
console.log(notAssigned); // Output: undefined
```

---

8. Null:

Represents the intentional absence of any object value.

Example:

```
let emptyValue = null;
console.log(emptyValue); // Output: null
```

Operators

An **Operator** is a symbol that is used to perform a mathematical or logical operation between variables or values (W3School, n.d.).

Here's the code snippet example I referenced in the *Variable section*:

```
var x = 5;

var y = 6;

var z = x + y;
```

The symbol = is used to represent the **assignment operator** which is used to assign values to a specific symbol. In this case, it is used to show that the **letter X** is equal to 5 and **letter Y** is equal to 6.

Also the assignment operator is used in conjunction with the **addition operator** + to show that the **letter *Z*** is equal to the sum of letters **X** and **Y**.

There are other *arithmetic operators* such as:

Arithmetic operators

1. Subtraction (-):

Description: Subtracts the right-hand operand from the left-hand operand.

Example:

```
let result = 10 - 5; // result is 5
```

Explanation: Here, `10 - 5` equals `5`. The `-` operator simply subtracts the right-hand operand value of `5` from the left-hand operand value of `10`.

---

2. Multiplication Operator (*)

Description: The multiplication operator is used to multiply two numbers.

Example:

```
let a = 6;

let b = 4;

let result = a * b; // Multiplies 6 by 4

console.log(result); // Output: 24
```

Explanation: Here, `6 * 4` equals `24`. The `*` operator simply multiplies the two numbers on either side of it.

---

3. Division (/):

Description: Divides the left-hand operand by the right-hand operand.

Example:

```
let result = 10 / 2; // result is 5
```

Explanation: Here, `10 / 2` equals `5`. The `/` operator simply divides the left-hand operand `10` by the right-hand operand `2`.

4. Modulus (`%`):

Description: Returns the remainder of the division between two numbers.

Example:
```
let result = 10 % 3; // result is 1
```

Explanation: Here, `10 % 3` equals `1`. The `%` operator simply divides the left-hand operand `10` by the right-hand operand `3`. Because `10` divided by `3` gives a remainder of `1` the answer is `1`

Comparison Operators

Comparison operators help you perform logical comparisons in your JavaScript code, allowing you to control the flow of execution based on conditions. Here they are:

1. Equality (==)

Description: Compares two values for equality after converting them to a common type (type coercion).

Example:
```
console.log(5 == '5'); // true
```

Here, the string '5' is converted to a number before comparison.

---

2. Inequality (`!=`)

Description: Compares two values for inequality after type coercion.

Example:
```
console.log(5 != '6'); // true
```

The values are not equal, so it returns true.

---

3. Strict Equality (`===`)

Description: Compares two values for equality without type conversion (no coercion).

Example:
```
console.log(5 === '5'); // false
```

Here, the comparison fails because the types (number vs. string) are different.

---

4. Strict Inequality (`!==`)

Description: Compares two values for inequality without type conversion.

Example:
```
console.log(5 !== '5'); // true
```

The values are not equal due to different types, so it returns true.

---

5. Less Than (`<`)

Description: Checks if the left operand is less than the right operand.

Example:
```
console.log(5 < 10); // true
```

---

6. Greater Than (`>`)

Description: Checks if the left operand is greater than the right operand.

Example:
```
console.log(10 > 5); // true
```

---

7. Less Than or Equal To (<=)

Description: Checks if the left operand is less than or equal to the right operand.

Example:
```
console.log(5 <= 5); // true
```

---

8. Greater Than or Equal To (>=)

Description: Checks if the left operand is greater than or equal to the right operand.

Example:
```
console.log(10 >= 5); // true
```

Summary

- == and != : Perform type coercion.
- === and !== : No type coercion; strict checks.
- <, >, <=, >=: Compare numerical values.

These operators help you perform logical comparisons in your JavaScript code, allowing you to control the flow of execution based on conditions.

Logical Operators

Logical operators are used to combine or invert boolean values. The three main logical operators are:

Logical AND (`&&`):

Description: This operator returns `true` if both operands are true.

Example:

```
const a = true;

const b = false;

const result = a && b; // result is false
```

Explanation: Here, result is `false` because both `a` and `b` must be true for the result to be `true`.

Logical OR (`||`):

Description: This operator returns `true` if at least one of the operands is true.

Example:

```
const a = true;

const b = false;

const result = a || b; // result is true
```

Explanation: In this case, result is `true` because `a` is true, so the overall expression evaluates to true.

Logical NOT (`!`):

Description: This operator inverts the boolean value of its operand.

Example:

```
const a = true;

const result = !a; // result is false
```

Explanation: Here, result is `false` because the NOT operator flips `true` to `false`.

Combining Logical Operators

You can also combine these operators to create more complex conditions:

```
const x = 5;

const y = 10;

const isGreater = (x > 3) && (y < 15); // isGreater is true

const isEither = (x < 3) || (y > 15); // isEither is false

const notTrue = !(x === 5); // notTrue is false
```

Explanation: In this example:

`isGreater is true` because both conditions are true.

`isEither is false` because neither condition is true.

`notTrue is false` because the expression `x === 5` is true, and the NOT operator inverts it.

These logical operators are fundamental in controlling the flow of your code, especially in conditional statements.

typeof Operator

The `typeof` operator in JavaScript is used to determine the type of a variable or an expression. It returns a string indicating the type. Here are some examples along with explanations:

Example 1: Basic Types

```
console.log(typeof "Hello, World!"); // "string"
```

```
console.log(typeof 42);                    // "number"

console.log(typeof true);                  // "boolean"

console.log(typeof undefined);             // "undefined"

console.log(typeof null);                  // "object" (this is a
known quirk in JavaScript)
```

Explanation:

- `typeof "Hello, World!"` returns `"string"` because it's a string value.
- `typeof 42` returns `"number"` since 42 is a numeric value.
- `typeof true` returns `"boolean"` because it's a boolean value.
- `typeof undefined` returns `"undefined"` when a variable has been declared but not assigned a value.
- `typeof null` returns `"object"` due to a historical bug in JavaScript.

Example 2: Complex Types

```
console.log(typeof { name: "Alice", age: 30 }); // "object"

console.log(typeof [1, 2, 3]);                   //
"object" (arrays are also objects)

console.log(typeof function() {});               // "function"

console.log(typeof new Date());                  // "object"
```

Explanation:

- `typeof { name: "Alice", age: 30 }` returns `"object"` because it's an object literal.
- `typeof [1, 2, 3]` returns `"object"` because arrays are technically objects in JavaScript.
- `typeof function() {}` returns `"function"` since functions are first-class objects.

- `typeof new Date()` returns `"object"` because a Date is also an object.

Example 3: Checking for Specific Types

```
let variable = "Hello";



if (typeof variable === "string") {

    console.log("It's a string!");

} else {

    console.log("It's not a string.");

}
```

Explanation: In this example, we check if `variable` is of type `"string"` using the `typeof` operator. If it is, we log "It's a string!". In this case the variable is `"Hello";` which is a string because it's letters so the console should log `It's a string!`

Summary

The `typeof` operator is useful for type checking and debugging, allowing developers to understand the data types they are working with in their code.

Bitwise XOR Operator

The ^ operator is a bitwise XOR (exclusive OR) operator. It compares two numbers on a bit level (binary) and returns 1 when the bits are different and 0 when they are the same.

Example:

```
let num1 = 5;  // Binary: 101
```

```
let num2 = 3;  // Binary: 011

let result = num1 ^ num2; // XOR: 110 (6 in decimal)

console.log(result); // Output: 6
```

Explanation:

- 5 in binary is `101`
- 3 in binary is `011`
- XOR compares the bits:
  - 1 ^ 0 = 1
  - 0 ^ 1 = 1
  - 1 ^ 0 = 0
- So the result is `110` (which is 6 in decimal).

Bitwise XOR can be useful in programming for various tasks, like:

- Finding differences between numbers.
- Swapping values without a temporary variable.
- Creating checksums for data verification.

As you can see, there is an operator to represent virtually every mathematical or logical operation.

Statements

Statements are lines of code that instruct the browser to perform a specific task or function. They are essentially a sequence of operators, values and expressions that are grouped together meant to be interpreted in a specific order or fashion (W3School, n.d.).

Here's an example of a statement (W3School, n.d.):

```
let x, y, z;

x = 7;
```

```
y = 3;

z = x + y;
```

As you can see the statement is used to instruct the browser on how to solve `Z = X + Y`, which based on the instruction should be `10`.

Expressions

An expression is an example of a *statement*, it is a combination of values, variables, and operators.

Essentially it is a sequence of calculations that lead to a unique value, like a number sentence such as; `5 + 3` = the value of `8` or `2*3` = the value of `6` (Brainstation, 2022).

Examples of expressions include arithmetic operations (you may recall these from the ***operators section***) such as `+` addition, `-` subtraction, `*` multiplication, and `/` division, as well as `&&` logical and `==` comparison operations.

As you can see from the examples, the symbols used in each expression are the same as the JavaScript operators mentioned earlier.

Functions

Functions are a code snippet that includes "procedures" or a set of statements and expressions that are grouped together for a specific purpose or to perform a task. Essentially they are meant to be used over and over again as opposed to creating a new function for every use (Brainstation, 2022).

Here's an example (W3Schools, n.d.):

```
function toCelsius(fahrenheit) {
  return (5/9) * (fahrenheit-32);
}
document.getElementById("demo").innerHTML = toCelsius(77);
```

The function includes several key parts:

```
function toCelsius(fahrenheit)
```

This statement identifies the function or procedure to be completed, in this case, the procedure is to convert Fahrenheit to Celsius.

Next part of the code snippet:

```
{
  return (5/9) * (fahrenheit-32);
}
```

This statement indicates the sequence of expressions to be completed in order to `return` the answer to the question.

Essentially the statement is saying to convert a Fahrenheit measurement to Celsius, the following steps must first be completed; Divide `5/9`, and take the inputted Fahrenheit measurement minus `-` `32`. Then take the result of these two expressions and multiply * them. As you can see the order in which these operations are performed is important in order to return the correct answer.

Then the last statement:

```
document.getElementById("demo").innerHTML = toCelsius(77);
```

Is instructing the computer to show the answer to the function on the user's screen via HTML more specifically as an HTML tag with the `id "demo"` (We will explore *DOM (Dynamic Object Model)* manipulation) in the next section.

The last part of the statement `toCelsius(77);` between the parentheses `()` is where the programmer would input the Fahrenheit number they wish to be converted.

In this case, the Fahrenheit number inputted was 77F. So the result should be 25C.

Again as you can see functions are great because they allow you to write reusable pieces of code. Instead of repeating yourself, you define a function and use it multiple times throughout your program.

DOM (Document Object Model) Manipulation

The **Document Object Model (DOM)** represents the structure of a webpage as a tree of objects. Each element on the page is part of this tree. JavaScript allows you to access and manipulate the DOM, which enables dynamic updates to the HTML content. As you can recall from the *functions section* with the Fahrenheit to Celsius function, we used DOM manipulation to show the answer to the function on the user's screen via HTML more specifically as an HTML tag with the `id "demo"`

Here are some more additional things you can do with DOM manipulation. For example, you can:

- Change the content of an element.
- Modify the styles dynamically.
- Add or remove elements from the page.

Let's look at another example of DOM manipulation in action:

```
document.getElementById("heading").innerHTML = "New Heading Text";
```

This line of JavaScript will change the content of an HTML element with the ID `heading` to `"New Heading Text"`. As you can see DOM manipulation is an excellent way to bring static webpages to life.

Events

An **Event** is a signal or alert that is triggered when users interact with an HTML element on a webpage (W3School, n.d.).

Essentially events are actions or occurrences that happen in the browser, like clicking a button, hovering over a link, or submitting a form. JavaScript allows you to "listen" for these events and respond to them.

Here's an example of an HTML code snippet that just uses the event `onlick` which tells the browser to trigger an event when a button `<button>` is clicked on:

```
<button onclick="displayDate()">The time is?</button>
```

This particular event is instructing the browser to display a date, when the `button` is clicked on (W3School, n.d.).

JavaScript can also listen for other events, such as `mouseover`, `keypress`, and `load`. As you can see, Events are a great way to build interactive web pages.

Conditional Statements

Conditional statements determine whether or not pieces of code can run, or if it is true or false. (W3Schools, n.d.). Essentially, you use them to execute code only if certain conditions are met.

There are three main types of conditional statements:

`if` statements: where if a condition is true it is used to specify execution for a block of code.

`else` statements: where if the same condition is false it specifies the execution for a block of code.

`else if` statements: this specifies a new test if the first condition is false.

Here's a code snippet example:

```
let num = 7;

if (num > 10) {
  console.log("The number is greater than 10.");
} else if (num > 5) {
  console.log("The number is greater than 5 but less than or equal
to 10.");
} else {
  console.log("The number is less than or equal to 5.");
}
```

The `let num = 7` indicates that the variable `num` will be assigned a value of `7`.

The `if` statement; `if (num > 10)` checks whether the value of the `num` variable is greater than `10`. If the statement is `true` then the text: `("The number is greater than 10.")` will be displayed on the user's console.

Since `num` is actually `7`, this condition is `false`, so the next statement `else if (num > 5)` will be executed instead.

If the statement is `true` for this piece of code, then the text: `("The number is greater than 5 but less than or equal to 10.")` will be displayed on the user's console.

But if the answer is `false`, then `else` statement is executed; if the value of `num` is less than `5`, then the console will instead log: `("The number is less than or equal to 5.")`

As you can see, Conditional statements are a significant part of JavaScript programming and are a great way to make the code more dynamic and responsive to user input or other changing conditions.

Loops

In JavaScript, loops are used to repeatedly execute a block of code as long as a specified condition is true. This allows you to automate repetitive tasks, iterate over data structures like arrays, or perform actions a set number of times. There are several types of loops in JavaScript:

1. `for` Loop

The `for` loop is commonly used when you know in advance how many times you want to iterate.

```
for (let i = 0; i < 5; i++) {
  console.log(i); // Output: 0, 1, 2, 3, 4
}
```

- **Initialization**: `let i = 0;` — This runs once at the start of the loop.
- **Condition**: `i < 5;` — The loop continues as long as this condition is true.

- **Increment/Update**: `i++` — This runs after each iteration.

---

2. `while` Loop

The `while` loop repeats as long as a specified condition is true.

```
let i = 0;

while (i < 5) {

  console.log(i);

  i++;

}
```

---

3. `do...while` Loop

The `do...while` loop is similar to the `while` loop, but it ensures that the loop runs at least once, even if the condition is initially false.

```
let i = 0;

do {

  console.log(i);

  i++;

} while (i < 5);
```

---

4. `for...of` Loop

This loop iterates over iterable objects like arrays, strings, or sets.

```
let array = [10, 20, 30];

for (let value of array) {
```

```
  console.log(value); // Output: 10, 20, 30

}
```

---

5. `for...in` Loop

This loop iterates over the keys of an object or an array's indices.

```
let obj = { a: 1, b: 2, c: 3 };

for (let key in obj) {

  console.log(key); // Output: a, b, c

}
```

Key Points:

- `for` is for a defined number of iterations.
- `while` is for conditional looping until the condition is false.
- `for...of` iterates over values of an iterable.
- `for...in` iterates over keys (properties or indices).

These looping mechanisms help to perform repetitive tasks efficiently in JavaScript.

Comments

To inform others about the instructions of the JavaScript code, developers are able to write **Comments**.

The comments also give the observer info on the **semantics** or the meaning of the code. (W3Schools, n.d.)
To indicate a single line comment, a user inputs double slashes //

Also any code that is between the slashes; / and / is treated as a comment also.

Lastly, according to W3Schools, a comment can also be used to stop a line of code from being executed, for testing purposes. (W3Schools, n.d.)

Here's an example of comments in action:

Code Snippet A: `let x = 5;    // I will be executed`

Code Snippet B: `// x = 6;    I will NOT be executed`

As you can see from the example, **Code Snippet A** will be executed, because the expression `let x = 5;` is included before the double slashes //. While **Code Snippet B** will not be executed because the expression `x = 6;` is not included before the double slashes.

Overall, JavaScript comments are pretty straight forward, and they are good to use when you need to provide information about what the code is being used for. Also if you want to stop a line of code from being executed so you can test the code.

In the next section we are going to explore the different ways in which JavaScript can be added to an HTML document. This will help you will be able to implement JavaScript yourself.

How JavaScript is Added to HTML

Similarly to CSS, JavaScript can be implemented on web pages in one of three ways:

1. Inline
2. External
3. Internally

Again, each has its own pros and cons.

Internal JavaScript

If JavaScript is written directly in an HTML document, a `<script>` tag in the `<head>` section of the document with the `language` and `type` attributes added indicates the code has been added.

Here's an example of a series of functions (Tutorialspoint, n.d.):

```
<head>
    <script language = "javascript" type = "text/javascript">
```

```
(function (w, d, s, l, i) {
        w[l] = w[l] || [];
        w[l].push({ "gtm.start": new Date().getTime(), event:
"gtm.js" });
        var f = d.getElementsByTagName(s)[0],
          j = d.createElement(s),
          dl = l != "dataLayer" ? "&l=" + l : "";
        j.async = true;
        j.src = "https://www.googletagmanager.com/gtm.js?id=" +
i + dl;
        f.parentNode.insertBefore(j, f);
      })(window, document, "script", "dataLayer", "GTM-
KVL636G");

     </script>
</head>
```

As you can see the code snippet is *nested* inside the `<head>` tags and the `language` and `type` attributes were added to the `<script>` tag to indicate that a JavaScript code snippet is being added.

The "code" nested in the `<script>` tag is an example of a *tracking pixel* which is a piece of JavaScript code used to track a webpage user's actions on the page.

Pros and Cons

Pros:

- Generally takes up less space

Cons:

- If in the `<head>` section it can slow down the webpage (render-blocking)
- May be harder to maintain and reuse code

External JavaScript

The code can also be loaded through an *external* file with the `.js` extension and then loading it within the page with again a `<script>` tag, and an `[src]` attribute added to the script tag, here's an example:

```
<body>
    <script src="name of file.js"></script>
</body>
```

The code does not necessarily need to be nested in the `<head>` tag. In this case, the code is being loaded from the `<body>` section of the HTML document.

Here are some pros and cons of external JavaScript, according to K.V. (2021):

Pros and Cons

Pros:

- Easy to reuse code.
- Easier to read
- Easier to compress and minify

Cons:

- The browser has to make an extra HTTP request to get the `.js` code.
- Code can be downloaded using the URL of the `.js` file. This can help coders to steal your code easily.
- If two `.js` files are dependent on one another, then a failure in one file may affect the execution of the other dependent file.
- A small change to a common `.js` file may cause unexpected results in some of the HTML files.

Inline JavaScript

Lastly, you can add the JavaScript code *inline* or directly inside an HTML tag, and then add **attributes** to the tag that trigger an action when interacted with such as:

- `onclick` (when the object is clicked on by the user)
- `onmouseover` (when the user moves their mouse)
- `onkeypress` (when the user presses a specific key on their keyboard)
- `onload` (when the user loads the webpage), etc.

These are also considered to be examples of **JavaScript Events** (recall the *Events section*)

Here's an example:

```
<button onclick="alert('Hello World!')">Click Me</button>
```

As you can see the attribute `onclick` was added with the action to show a display box with the text "Hello world" when the button is clicked on (Tutorial Republic n.d.).

Here are the Pros and Cons for this method:

Pros and Cons

Pros:

- Generally takes up less space

Cons:

- Harder to maintain code
- Difficult to reuse code for other projects
- Unable to be *cached* or saved for future use by Web Browsers

Last Words About JavaScript

JavaScript is an essential tool for every web developer. It allows you to go beyond static content and create engaging, interactive websites that respond to user input.

Whether it's adding a simple button click event or building an entire web application, JavaScript is the key to unlocking dynamic functionality on the web.

Chapter 5: Mastering HTML, CSS, and JavaScript Through Projects

When it comes to mastering these coding languages, building projects allows you to apply what you've learned, tackle real-world problems, and improve your coding skills incrementally.

In this chapter, we'll discuss some excellent projects that will help you master these core web technologies. These projects cover a range of difficulty levels, from beginner to advanced, and offer opportunities to apply HTML, CSS, and JavaScript creatively.

Also I included links to websites with project templates, at the time of writing the book the links were valid, but if they are not a simple search engine search will help you find these projects. Also, please note, I am not affiliated, nor endorsing any of the websites/web authors mentioned, these were just the top most results that I found on Google.

1. Personal Portfolio Website:

Every web developer should start with a personal portfolio. This project allows you to practice basic HTML structure, semantics, and accessibility while showcasing your work.

A portfolio site is a perfect playground to explore responsive design techniques with CSS, including Flexbox and Grid. You can also add simple interactivity with JavaScript, like toggling a dark mode or creating a dynamic project gallery.

Key Skills Developed:

- Semantic HTML for search engines and accessibility
- CSS layouts (Flexbox, Grid, Media Queries)
- Basic JavaScript interactions (modals, buttons, animations)
- SEO best practices through metadata and structured data

Resources and Links

- https://www.geeksforgeeks.org/how-to-create-a-portfolio-website-using-html-css-and-javascript/
- https://github.com/topics/responsive-portfolio-website
- https://codewithcurious.com/projects/personal-portfolio-using-html-css-js/

2. Responsive Landing Page:

Building a landing page for a product or service is a great way to challenge yourself with layout techniques and CSS responsiveness. This project requires attention to both design and functionality.

It's an opportunity to work with forms, navigation menus, and call-to-action buttons, all while ensuring the site looks great on any screen size.

Key Skills Developed:

- Mobile-first design and media queries for responsive layouts
- CSS transitions and animations for a more polished user experience
- HTML form handling
- Browser compatibility and debugging techniques

Resources and Links

- https://www.geeksforgeeks.org/how-to-create-a-landing-page-using-html-css-and-javascript/
- https://dev.to/ananiket/create-a-responsive-landing-page-using-html-css-js-b7m
- https://www.freecodecamp.org/news/how-to-make-a-landing-page-with-html-css-and-javascript/

3. Interactive Quiz App:

Creating a quiz app is an excellent way to dive deeper into JavaScript. You'll need to work on data management, event handling, and DOM manipulation.

A quiz app can be as simple or complex as you like. Start by building a basic quiz that tracks scores, displays questions, and provides feedback to the user. Then, improve it by adding features like saving progress, using localStorage, or making it a timed quiz.

Key Skills Developed:

- JavaScript event listeners and DOM manipulation
- Data handling with arrays and objects
- Dynamic HTML generation

- CSS styling for a clean, usable interface

Resources and Links

- https://www.geeksforgeeks.org/create-a-quiz-app-with-timer-using-html-css-and-javascript/
- https://www.codewithfaraz.com/content/161/build-a-quiz-application-with-html-css-and-javascript-step-by-step-guide
- https://medium.com/@dinithinethmini01/build-a-quiz-application-with-html-css-and-javascript-3cac01e848e7

4. JavaScript Game (e.g., Tic-Tac-Toe or Memory Game):

Creating a small browser-based game is both fun and challenging. Games like Tic-Tac-Toe, Memory, or Snake are excellent projects for improving your JavaScript logic.

You'll need to work on game state management, user input handling, and perhaps even basic AI for computer-controlled opponents. Games are also great for practicing CSS animations to enhance user experience.

Key Skills Developed:

- Complex JavaScript logic and conditional statements
- Managing game state with JavaScript
- CSS animations for smooth gameplay
- Enhancing interactivity with sound effects or visual feedback

Resources and Links

- https://www.geeksforgeeks.org/simple-tic-tac-toe-game-using-javascript/
- https://marina-ferreira.github.io/tutorials/js/memory-game/

5. E-commerce Product Page:

Designing a mock product page for an e-commerce site is a project that brings together multiple disciplines. You can focus on creating a highly optimized, responsive layout that mimics real-world e-commerce sites.

Adding JavaScript functionalities such as image carousels, product quantity selection, and dynamic pricing calculations helps to simulate a user-friendly online shopping experience.

Key Skills Developed:

- HTML for complex page layouts (e.g., product descriptions, reviews, etc.)
- CSS for responsive design and user interface
- JavaScript for dynamic price updates, product filters, or image galleries
- SEO considerations like structured data and content optimization

Resources and Links

- https://www.frontendmentor.io/solutions/responsive-ecommerce-product-page-using-html-css-and-javascript-qC1XmCWswm
- https://codewithcurious.com/projects/ecommerce-website-using-html-css-js/
- https://dev.to/themodernweb/how-to-make-an-e-commerce-website-with-html-css-and-js-3aon

6. Blog Platform:

A simple blog platform is a more advanced project, combining your knowledge of HTML, CSS, and JavaScript into one cohesive application.

It requires you to create multiple pages, use forms for user-generated content (like comments), and manage data either through localStorage or by simulating a back-end with static JSON files. You can even extend this project into a full-stack application later by learning about back-end technologies.

Key Skills Developed:

- Multi-page site structure and navigation
- Working with JavaScript to manage and display blog posts dynamically
- Handling user input and comments
- Designing for readability and accessibility

Resources and Links

- https://www.geeksforgeeks.org/blog-website-using-javascript/

- https://dev.to/themodernweb/fullstack-how-to-create-a-working-blogging-website-with-pure-html-css-and-js-in-2021-9di
- https://github.com/kunaal438/blogging-site

7. Photo Gallery with Lightbox Effect:

A photo gallery is an aesthetically pleasing project that allows you to explore both front-end design and dynamic interaction. A lightbox effect can be implemented with JavaScript to highlight images when clicked, making the user experience more immersive. You can also add features like image filters, tags, and sorting options to enhance functionality.

Key Skills Developed:

- CSS for grid-based layouts and hover effects
- JavaScript for lightbox interactions and image filtering
- Optimizing images for web performance
- Ensuring mobile responsiveness and fast load times

Resources and Links

- https://www.geeksforgeeks.org/how-to-create-image-lightbox-gallery-using-html-css-and-javascript/
- https://www.codingnepalweb.com/image-gallery-lightbox-html-css-javascript/
- https://medium.com/@modhupromz01/creating-an-image-gallery-with-hover-effect-and-lightbox-in-html-css-and-javascript-d31da28b8970

Final Thoughts

The projects outlined in this chapter serve as a roadmap for mastering HTML, CSS, and JavaScript. Each project tackles different aspects of web development, from responsive design and accessibility to dynamic user interfaces.

Whether you're just starting or advancing your skills, these projects will help you gain confidence in your abilities and develop a portfolio that showcases your knowledge of web development best practices.

By completing these projects, you'll gain not only technical skills but also the problem-solving mindset essential for success in web development. The more you experiment with different layouts, structures, and interactions, the more versatile and efficient you'll become in crafting effective web solutions.

Chapter 6: Continuing The Journey

As we come to the conclusion of this journey, it's important to step back and reflect on what you've learned about the fundamental building blocks of web development—**HTML, CSS**, and **JavaScript**. These three technologies are the backbone of every website, each playing a vital role in how a page is structured, styled, and brought to life.

HTML: The Structure of the Web

Think of HTML (Hypertext Markup Language) as the skeleton of a webpage. It's the foundational language that defines the structure and content. Every element you see on a webpage—headings, paragraphs, images, links—are all defined by HTML. It creates the framework that tells browsers what content is on the page and how it's organized.

By learning HTML, you've acquired the ability to structure content in a logical, hierarchical way. You've learned about different elements, how to create forms, tables, and lists, and how to link to other web pages. These are the basic tools that allow you to create the framework of any website.

CSS: Designing the Web

While HTML defines the structure, CSS (Cascading Style Sheets) brings style and design to the page. It's the language that makes websites visually appealing. With CSS, you've explored the power of colors, typography, spacing, and layout. You've discovered how to transform a plain page into something visually engaging, how to create responsive designs that adjust to different screen sizes, and how to enhance the user experience with smooth animations.

Mastering CSS allows you to take control of your designs, ensuring that your websites look polished and professional. The flexibility and creativity CSS offers are almost limitless, giving you the ability to experiment with aesthetics and layouts to achieve the desired impact.

JavaScript: Interactivity and Dynamics

JavaScript adds a layer of interactivity and functionality to your web pages. While HTML and CSS are static, JavaScript allows for dynamic behavior. With it, you've unlocked the potential to create websites that respond to user input, perform calculations, update content in real time, and interact with external data sources.

JavaScript is a versatile language that can do everything from creating interactive forms to building full-scale applications. By learning the basics, you've started on a path that opens the door to more advanced programming concepts like APIs, frameworks, and libraries. JavaScript bridges the gap between static content and dynamic experiences, empowering you to bring life to your web pages.

Last Words

Web development is a creative and technical journey that doesn't end here. Now that you've built a solid foundation, the key is to keep experimenting, learning, and pushing your skills. With these core principles in hand, you're ready to dive deeper into more complex challenges and explore new technologies.

Whether you build personal projects, contribute to open-source communities, or continue learning through courses and resources, the opportunities are endless. The more you practice and apply what you've learned, the more confident and proficient you will become.

As you move forward, remember that the web is a dynamic environment where curiosity and creativity thrive. You now have the ability to create, innovate, and transform ideas into digital reality. Embrace the process, enjoy the learning, and continue building the web of tomorrow.

Good luck, and happy coding!

Continued Readings

Learning front-end web development is only half the battle to producing an amazing web experience. Also you need to learn **SEO (search engine optimization)**.

Learning SEO ensures that visitors can actually find your website, and apps on the internet. Below I included links to several SEO books I've written. They are excellent reads.

The ABCs of SEO: Search Engine Optimization 101

https://www.amazon.com/ABCs-Search-Engine-Optimization-Page-ebook/dp/B0C2JSLW7M

The Technical SEO Handbook

https://www.amazon.com/Technical-SEO-Handbook-Learn-Issues-ebook/dp/B0CMBJR9QV

The SEO and Web Developer Collaboration Guide

https://www.amazon.com/SEO-Web-Developer-Collaboration-Guide-ebook/dp/B0DHLBM48C

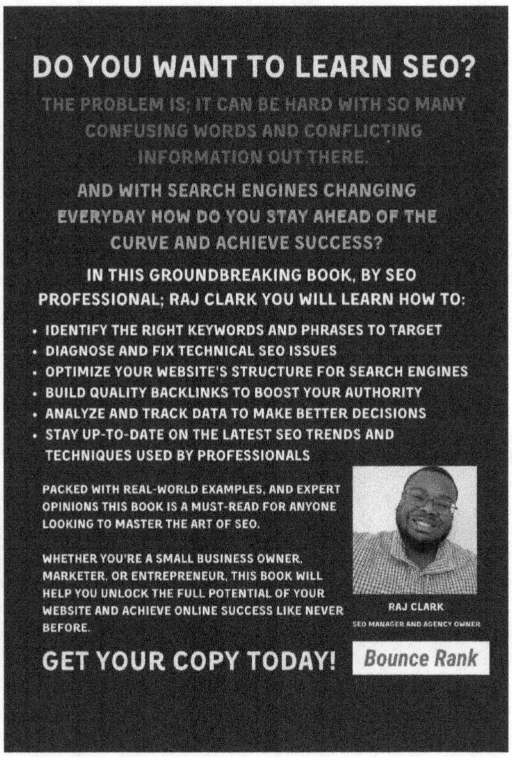

About the Author

Roggie (Raj) Clark, is a 9 year SEO professional and owner of the SEO agency; *Bounce Rank.* Prior to joining the SEO industry, Raj was a web developer and school teacher. It was through creating his own websites, and wanting a career change from teaching, that Raj stumbled across the world of SEO.

Since joining the field nearly a decade ago, Raj has worked on a wide range of campaigns, from eCommerce, to B2B, to Healthcare, for enterprise companies and marketing agencies in the United States.

He is regarded as an expert, and guru by his colleagues, and the SEO industry. Raj currently lives in Maryland with his sister and niece.

About the Author

www.ingramcontent.com/pod-product-compliance
Lightning Source LLC
LaVergne TN
LVHW082358200926
848481LV00012B/3611